Why ice cream trucks play Christmas songs

Paul Jolly

Fernwood
PRESS

Why ice cream trucks play Christmas songs

Fernwood Press
Newberg, Oregon
www.fernwoodpress.com

"Elected" first appeared in the Columbia Journal.

Cover image by Joanna Axtmann,
"Auspicious Doors #3 - shell doors,"
joannaaxtmann.com

Printed in the United States of America

ISBN 978-1-59498-053-4

for Anna
and in memory of Robert Jolly (1926–2016)

Contents

The First Trip

Safe harbor

Did you ever finish a puzzle except one piece
and the piece in your hand didn't fit the hole?

Did you ever finish a puzzle except one piece
and what's in your hand wasn't even a puzzle piece—

but a long-preserved seed of a near-extinct melon?
Did you ever carve a melon into a boat with a message

chiseled into the rind and send it downstream?
The message promises: Newton's first law of motion

does not apply to you. Yes, things
keep moving the same direction, but you

can change from the course your mother and father
choose. The boy who found the melon message

—Aaron is his name—is now grown up. He finds
you and asks about the message. You

and Aaron sit near the melon patch with your feet
in the stream and talk about missing puzzle

pieces, and entire missing puzzles, and the potency
of near-extinct melon seeds, and other

things Newton knew nothing about. You
both laugh that Newton's pockets of ignorance

cause almost as much joy as your own spacious
pockets of ignorance and the ignorance of your radiant,

generous parents.

The children's fantasy land grab

Disney's scouts loiter at the rabbit hole.
Hands in pockets, they finger bundles of cash.
"Hey," they call to Alice, "how far down…" She
dives after the rabbit without answer.

Disney's scouts follow Wendy to Neverland
flying with wobbly technique and stolen fairy dust.
They promise guns to Captain Hook, ignorant
of the delicate Hook / Pan power balance.

Disney's scouts ask Eeyore who owns the Hundred
Acre Wood. He launches a screed about trampled
thistles. They imagine Christopher
Robin a hard bitten real estate tycoon.

One of Disney's scouts has a blue bruise on his cheek.
Mary Poppins walloped him with her umbrella
when he tried to help her across the street.
"Try to help a lady," he says mournfully.

Disney scouts sit in the little wooden
children's room chairs, try aimless chatter
with a suspicious librarian about The Hot
New Neighborhood. Location, location.

Disney won't be pleased when they return to HQ
with no intel. He'll whine: the money he pays them,
the Expensive Suits advance, the cost of gasoline,
cartoonists with pencils poised, storyless one more day.

Talent show at the old folks' home

The emphasemiac takes his tuba from its case
and taps a brisk rhythm on his wheelchair footrest.
He inhales carefully and lifts the brass coil to his lips.

The former ballroom dancer cradles the ghost of his wife
and partner of five decades in his amputated arms. His perfect
posture is a memorial to her beauty.

The pool shark, after years of blindness, has mastered
in his mind the break that sinks six balls, all solids.
"Ricochet," he explains, smiling.

Amazingly, in spite of Parkinson's, gyroscopes haywire,
the knife thrower sometimes hits his target.

Player piano

Player piano in the empty funeral parlor foyer cranks
out old standards with a Dixieland flourish. The old
wooden cross. How great thou art. Take my hand precious
Lord. No one hears it. No one is here to discuss pre-planning.

No one peruses coffins for his aunt who has been sick so long
the family forgot she would die. No one is scooped out
by grief at the accidental death of her husband who had
been sleeping in the guest room for years, and came back

to bed a week ago. No one stacks pride on top of patriotism
to crush the epileptic rage when his son is sent home,
done in by friendly fire. The embalming room is empty
glistening with germicide. In the whole town, it's a small town,

but still, the whole day, no one dies, no one talks about death,
death troubles no one's tranquility. The mortician drums
his plump fingers on his desk, keeping time to the old
favorites played by no one, that only he can hear.

There is a later train

This isn't the last train. But the late train
has no quiet cars. If a baby squalls no conductor
shushes her. You must shush her yourself.
The late train has no dining car. So board

this train now, or pack a picnic, your own
tablecloth, napkins, napkin-rings, silver,
porcelain. The late train has no schedule.
Depends on how many girlfriends the brakeman

wants to visit, how fast each girlfriend
forgives him, how long each visit lasts.
This is the last express train. The late train
switches engines at each depot, refuels

at every coal yard, stops to grease axels
before each switch. Sometimes it just stops.
The conductor on the late train is corrupt
and will demand a bribe, a surcharge, a handling

fee, a remittance. Take extra coins and know
your suitcase will be ransacked for cash.
The late train is segregated. Uphill
rules: Bare heads in odd rows. Hatted

or scarved people in even rows.
Oldies left of aisle, youngsters
to the right. Women in window
seats. Men in aisle seats. Citizens

in the front of the car. Immigrants at the back.
Down-slope, it's all reversed. Hooligan
conductors will evict anyone
in the wrong spot. Not evict from seat,

evict from train. Is this train going to heaven?
Yes. Is the late train going to heaven?
Yes. It's simpler to say "All aboard.
This is the last train." The evangelists'

workbook has pictures of people stranded
on the platform. The word nuance does not appear
in the evangelists' workbook. I am writing a new
version of the book. It's much longer.

New chapters, footnotes, caveats, disclaimers,
counterclaims, exceptions, cross-references.
No absolutes. No strict dichotomies.
Still, you should get on this train.

Bubble milk tea

Bubble milk tea is the rage of the decade.
Dairy farmers double-pump udders
to fulfill bubble milk demand.
They pump gas through a cow's
four stomachs and the milk
comes out carbonated. Steep
the tea an extra minute to match
the milk's fortitude. Some tea
shops cheat and spritz milk
through the soda fizzer. But a drinker
can tell the diff. Milk that's bubbled
in the cow just tastes better.

Brits and other tea purists are scandalized.
Still feeling zinged by red zinger
and other herbal upstarts.

Greedy farmers over-inflate cows. Cows
float away. Farmers scan the back pages
of their livestock insurance policies. No luck.
Bubble cow floatation is an act of God.

The trend causes controversy
and consternation from the usual
controverters and consternators.

At the waffle shop in town, farmers take
umbrage. They take it hard. Enviro-grumps
growl about cow pollution. On the contrary.
Bubble milk solves global warming,
redirects methane from fart-valve
to milk-valve. Animal rights activists insist
it hurts the cows. On the contrary. Cows
giggle when gasified. Those nutbars
want cows back to their natural habitat.
Someone please explain to them
that a cow's natural habitat is halfway
down a wolf's gullet. Every poll,
ninety-nine percent of cows prefer
the farm and bubbles in your four
tummies is an extra bonus.

The day before the croquet match

Clubs, ace to king, prepare for a day of wicketness.
Yoga (downward dog) helps. Limbering ointment
promises more flex, less ache. If cards crease, it's

Off with their heads!

Diamonds are dispatched to capture
hedgehogs. They trek into the woods with hedgehog
horns and nets. Problem is, hedgehogs who've played
croquet past years are not invited for rematch.
The moment the flamingo-mallet strikes, they recoil,
uncurl. It's near dusk, and all the hedgehogs
found so far sport disqualifying pink
feathers in their quills. If the hunters slump
back to the palace with empty nets, it's

Off with their heads!

Spades march marshward to procure flamingos.
Same problem. Birds that have played croquet
flinch at the moment of contact. A shell-shocked
flamingo with quilled jowls can't play croquet.
If spades return with flamingo wagon vacant, it's

Off with their heads!

The croquet court is lined with white rose bushes.
Her Maj. wants red roses so paint buckets are passed
around. Ten hearts and one joker paint white roses red.
Their Maj's are exempted, and Jack's in jail on a tart
snatch charge. They work fast and reckless. Splotch
and drip of red on a leaf, paint streaks on the grass,
one tipped-over paint bucket. No doubt it's

Off with their heads!

It's up to you, Alice. Be bold. Due process trashed.
All four suits face genocide. Hedgehogs and flamingos
on the doorknock of extinction. Roses screwed
by lead poisoning. Things get so far off whack,
it takes supernatural reach to yank
them back. You are the supernat. Exert.

Pig on trial

It's hard to live a making, hard, hard to make a living
even without the exorcist interferes. I've been a fog
harmer, a hog harmer. I have hogged farms all my life
and my father's life before that. I'm so mad I can't talk right
and the priest will probably say I'm witch crafted too.

I've already paid the lawyer more than the pork
is worth. The lawyers available to represent pigs no
longer take pork for payment. The bailiff can't find
an oink-to-English translator. The trig is riled. The whole
trial is rigged. Priest wants to know did the pig confess?

Is the pig penitent? Penitent is not in a pig
vocabulary. I know it's the church's job to root
out demons. This pig is bad, deserves to die.
But don't hurt my family. My children are good.
The barnyard demon didn't enter the house.

Hogwash

The last domestic hogwash firm
closed its last American plant.
It's not a high profit margin product,
but you can't wash hogs without it.
Import tariffs force prices up steep.

Some farmers try plain soap. Their hogs
develop folliculitis and unsightly
blisters. Customers are disgusted.

Some pay outlandish prices for foreign
hogwash and try to charge premium for clean
skin pork. Customers aren't persuaded.

Some hog farmers wring their hands
and say, "Wee wee wee," kvetching,
moaning and bemoaning the outsource,
off-shore, agro-biz, global monopolizers.

The successes are farmers who craft their own
small batch hogwash, family formulas five
generations old. Hogwash, they say, is
hogwash, worthless unless you got none.

An army marches on its stomach

Little known fact: Napoleon was an amateur
naturalist. When he said, "An army marches
on its stomach," he meant an army of gastropods,
his special curiosity. A squadron of slugs

advances through the forest. The sergeant
is silent. The usual "Left, Right, Left"
would embarrass the troops. After a punishing
three-meter march, they spy the enemy

in the clearing. A platoon of snails
reads letters from home and rolls cigarettes.
One slug scout is fitted with a snail
shell disguise and dispatched to learn

the snails' battle plans. A blade of grass
knocks loose his badly attached shell.
The crazed snails salt him but he keeps
bravely mum. His comrades retreat

to their bivouac in the woods. They pass
a bottle of champagne, mourn their fallen
hero and dedicate next day's battle
to his valor. Napoleon knows

an army marches on it stomach.
He insists on feasting his troops after
the long march and grief. No hard tack.
No tinned meat. Turtle soup, quail eggs,

caviar, foie gras, *fromage*, more champagne.
With especial gusto, they lift the lid
from the cast iron pot nested in the coals,
inhale garlic, and devour escargot.

Why ice cream trucks play Christmas songs

We three kings had a fleece as white as snow.
Twinkle twinkle little star, won't you guide my sleigh
tonight? Puff the magic dragon you better not cry.
It's the middle of mid Atlantic swelter—sweat drips

down each spine and every temple, but the faux
-calliope on the van plays Christmas songs. Just
when a humidity-flogged body can't recall
ever being chilled, popsicles, drum sticks, ice

cream sandwiches. Throat-lump cold plastic-wrapped.
This truck claims the same mythic zone as a winter
solstice bonfire. It's the zig-zag in the yin yang.
Each heat stroke holds the seeds of hypothermia.

Each beach blanket bingo holds the seeds of a white
Christmas sleigh ride. The corn is as high as the fourth
of July and a sleigh and eight reindeer fly
across the sky. The ice cream truck man is off

season Santa. Give him two dollars for a soft serve
cone that will drip before it reaches your lips.
The cantilever of the seasons. Counterbalance
of creation. Happy heat wave to all, and to all a good night.

Grant's ball cap stays put

Grant drops his ball cap on the doormat when he leaves
home in a seven AM fumbling fuss:
keys, bookbag, lunch-bucket, coat, gloves.

At noon a wind gust blusters. It snatches dead
branches from Grant's tree, shuttles yesterday's paper
down gutter from corner to corner, frees a kite

jammed in the joists and girders of a skyscraper
in progress. Several hats are lifted from heads.
An updraft cascade of fedoras, panamas,

and homburgs blackens the horizon.
One Stetson off a visiting Texan. A stovepipe
from an earlier century. Safari hats, bowlers

and boaters clutter skyways, get sucked into jet
engines, helpless as ducks, endanger passengers
and try the prowess of pilots. But Grant's hat

is on the mat when he steps off the bus at dusk.
Grant's joy ripples from shoelaces to fingertips,
strums his rib cage's corrugation, blossoms

in a smile and tickles his scalp. Thank you hat. Thank you
home. Thank you cup, water, steam, teabag, chair.
Grant sleeps capped and wakes gratitude-wrapped.

Your confirmation number begins with twelve zeros

I called 1-800-please-hold and sat through
a twenty minute medley of old favorites. The next
available agent fixed my problem, and then
said, Your confirmation number begins
with twelve zeros. I was so vexed, I didn't
hear the other digits. That's what's wrong

with corporate America! A dozen goose eggs,
and it wasn't even a golden goose. Slap
a one in front of those zeros and it's
a trillion. Do you know how long this phone call
would last if I counted to a trillion?

You wouldn't be so cavalier about zero
if you respected history. Hundreds of years
the Silk Route trade thrived—mirrors
exchanged for silk, swords swapped
for nutmeg—without a single zero.
Ninth century Indian mathematicians fretted
sleepless nights about this number
that wouldn't sit on the bottom of a fraction.
Five hundred years ago travelers
from India to Persia brought
the zero. With chess. And salami.

And leap year. And glass-lens telescopes.
When zero arrived in Europe no one
knew what to do with it. Even today:

school children are taught You can't
divide by zero with the same absolute
arbitrary authority as You can't cut in line, and
Raise your hand if you have something to say.

A zero is a quandary that crafts its own
mystery arithmetic. It demands respect.
I know that this call is being monitored
for quality and training purposes. Here is all
the quality and training I can muster: please
promise you will not abuse zero any more.

Yes, you have resolved the issue I called
about. But you raised so many other
issues we didn't have time to discuss.
Just promise. No more zero abuse.

Gathering Axel's bones

Grave robbers and twice-damned excommunicated
priests shaved shards off the skeleton of my favorite
saint Axel. A quick coin in the extra-clerical healers' world.
The pious still buy what grave-robbing relic-mongers sell.

When Constantinople went heathen, frescoes
and mosaics in every church were painted over.
The reliquary with a sliver of Saint Axel's clavicle
was shuffled out the side door and delivered
by camel to safety at a cliff-clutching Armenian
monastery. The Patriarch has been instructed:
the minute the last monk dies send me that sliver.

In Nueva España, a lone Jesuit evangelist, three
quarters starved, stumbled from where his horse
fell. Tucked in the folds of his cassock a chip
of Saint Axel's femur that he showed locals
to persuade them of the afterlife. Bishop Armando
of Coahuila promised he will ship me that chip.

A Portuguese pirate demanded payment from each
ship that crossed the Mediterranean: Genoan,
Ottoman, he didn't care. Impervious, he said,
to cannon because he braided a splinter of Saint Axel's
finger bone in his hair. I've hired divers to find the bone.

When the Cajuns uprooted from the rocky Atlantic
coast and trekked to the Mississippi's mushy banks
one man sewed a splinter of saint Axel's spine
into the hem of his canvass ruck sack. He said
the relic protected the band from malaria.
I have scoured the local history museums of half
Louisiana's parishes to find the splinter.

Any spirit whose carcass was so maltreated
must be raw, restless, disgruntled. Axel
is credited with a lifetime's miracles, more
miracles after death. I want to collect all
shards, splinters, fragments in one coffin. Ask
no more tricks, healings, reconcilings. Pray
your own prayers. Do your own work.

The Monkey Shakespeare Proof

Infinite numbers of monkeys
bang on typewriters for all
eternity. One produces
Hamlet. So the theory goes.

It takes infinite motivational
M&Ms and an infinite
number of clipboard-clutching
graduate students

to clean the saliva and other
fluids off the keys. And infinite
earnest Humane Society monitors
who threaten shrill scolding

at the first whiff of cruelty. Costly
research, no benefit to humanity.
We already have Hamlet.
But consider the thrill as one

monkey pounds out the first
scene: ghost and fog! He keeps
typing—the villainy of Uncle
King-Murderer is revealed!

The scientists crowd around,
tossing not just M&Ms
but whole one-dollar
candy bars at the lucky or smart

monkey. The press is alerted.
Linguists and lit profs ponder
what Shakespeare would think.
Rosencrantz and Guildenstern

collude with the evil monarch, check.
Hamlet offs the windbag Polonius, check.
Ophelia drowns, check. Statisticians
excitedly explain probability to bored

talk show hosts. Bodies pile up on stage
in Act Five, check, check, check.
Laertes skewers Hamlet, and the monkey
—the first nonhuman nominee

to the Mathematicians' Hall of Fame
—types Horatio's farewell: "Good
night sweet prince, and flights
of angels sing thee to thy resbobklimpf."

Scientists who were oddly exuberant
resume sobriety. "We still
have infinite monkeys," they say,
"and eternity is a long, long, time."

Beyond Abracadabra

Quintus Samonicus Serenus, third century Roman
doctor, master of the healing strength of Abracadabra,
owned sixty thousand books. Why? Why did a master

of Abracadabra covet more wisdom? He might
have acquired his library *before* the mystic
from the East gave him the five-syllable

mantra, and kept it to honor his father's
expansive mind. Or perhaps he bought
the books from pushcart merchants because

their look added luster to his practice and allowed
him to charge extra for his abracadabrafications.
Maybe he thought one of those books

held another incantation as potent
as the A-word, the key to endless wealth,
world fame, permanent prestige. Or, could be,

his secret concubine, his wife's hair-comber
and mascara tracer, was the reader in the house.
She gave him a deal: access to her dark,

warm place in exchange for access
to his stacks of books, each the knob
of a door that opens to reveal its own world.

Testosterone pockets

In places where testosterone pools,
puddles of piss and petroleum,
men gather. Their unapologetic
maleness bulges and sags and settles.

VFW halls, volunteer fire stations, delis
where nine-fingered butchers man
the meat slicer, body shops with Saturday
afternoon small town young bucks

slouched around hot rods, cigar lounges
in downtown clubs, gyms where broken
boxers limp and brag to aspiring featherweights.
There is power in these vectors of guydom.

Collective porn fantasies pop up. Visions of giggling,
eager-to-please, eager-to-strip bombshells reaching
for belt-buckles. Dull-witted dudes experience
perfect recall, decades of sports scores. They talk

without pause or shame about the balletic art
of the game. At these vortexes of manhood, beer gushes
from the cracked earth. No one explains anything.
A man can say "it is what it is" and everyone nods.

Wrong totem, maybe wrong mushroom

Alpha beasts know me. I'm on a first-name
basis with food chain pinnacle predators.
I wade with Uncle Grizzly to swat upstream

-leaping salmon out of the air. Brother Wolf
calls me across canyons. I tip my wings
to catch updraft with Cousin Eagle, trace

circles in the sky. We are the majestic
carnivores: different species, same
rank. I commune with swaggerers.

So I'm baffled, shaman, by my quote familiar
unquote. I fasted three days, walked
on the fourth day upstream to the deep

pool, bathed, scrambled up the sacred
escarpment, ate mushroom, slept, dreamt
a scaly-tailed possum. Did I munch the wrong

mushroom? I deserve a fierce totem. My ideal
companion is a venomous or constricting
snake. Yes, I know possums are North America's

only marsupial. I watched the National Geo
special. Big deal. It looks like an eight
pound rat, road-kill prone. It's not me.

Rehabilitate

Jerome the unprayed-to saint-in-waiting
didn't care if he was canonized. But now
amnesia softens the mind of his earthly
miracles' sole surviving witness. Jerome
suffers panic, wist surges and rage spikes.

He looks down from a tippy stool in a lonely
corner of heaven, pleading: someone call
my name. Jerome wants to give back.
He's a moldy-bored freelance Triple-A tow
truck driver whose dispatch is silent.

The meek may inherit the earth, but heaven
belongs to the bold. If the beneficiary
of the miracle is a shapely believer on doubt
-brink, even better. After a celibate life,
he anticipates a lusty afterlife. He can deliver

her of a burning house, whispering catechisms.
Her arms circle his neck, her knees grip his waist,
chaste flannel nighty hiked up. Maybe a painter
will capture his moment. A painter with one
studio for church-worthy works, one for smut.

Potato spirit is the thing

Edward craved Wilhelm's covet for his bus-length auto.
Stiff nod, audible inhale, man-to-man shoulder punch
would do. The war to end all wars didn't have to happen.

But the monomaniacal monarch had to brag his race
car fuel know-how. How did porcelain ego family
squabble turn to trench warfare? The so-called

chemists were as brusque as the emperor. They toiled
and tinkered with their potato concoction, drove
the scullery maids to quit. From that tick of Buckingham

Palace's grandfather clock, war was certain. Both courts'
protocol experts pleaded for peace. Failed. Polished
bureaucrats failed. Self-boring dukes and lords failed.

Generals protested. Failed. The Buckingham Palace
scullery maids even promised to return to their sinks
to save their brothers and boyfriends from bloodspill.

But Victoria's offsprung, some hemophiliacs meaning
uncoagulant, all hemophiliac meaning bloodlover,
were girding the loins of conscripts. I want to wake

Wilhelm from the grave, shake the dirt from
his skeletal earholes and shout: "You can
save seventeen million lives. Potato spirit is not

the thing. The Buckingham Palace scullery maids need to scull. Be a nephew. Apologize. Call off your chemists. Admire the damned car."

Goats deserve justice

The only time goats show up in the gospels
is when they are separated from sheep
on judgment day. What's up with that?
The sideways-chewing, cross-eyed, bloat-bellied,
callous-kneed creatures that no one loves

but their creator and their goat mamas. Goat mamas
can only love one litter at a time, and now you tell me
the Almighty, on the day of judgment, on the big
day, will turn his omnipotent back?
Can't he love a sheep without hating a goat?

On the day of reckoning, why not judge
each goat by its own misbehavior?
They deserve their tribunals, each cantankerous
member of the family Capra. Sure, they are all
stone-headed, but the final bell

has not rung. Listen to the soaring tenor
solo in the goat church choir—don't
you want that creature in heaven's chorus?
Watch for the kneeling penitent goat,
eyes cast demurely down, promising

to be good, and really, really meaning it
this time. All I ask is that you list each
goat separately in the book—Tulip,
Monkey, Junkyard, all of them—and hear
their stories, their defenses, their excuses.

Rub a dub dub

Three fat craftsmen, knee
to knee in a vat, bail bilge.
Throw them out, knaves all three,
Mother Goose demanded. Knaves

sounds vaguely sinister. But their crime
is not recorded. Yes the candles sputter
and spark. Yes the butcher was named
in the horse hoof in the pork sausage

scandal. Yes the baker sleeps through delivery
most mornings. But to sentence them to sink
in a rudderless bucket is harsh.
Why is Mother Goose vindictive?

The silly rhymes mask a vengeful soul.
Kids love Bo Peep, Miss Muffett,
Humpty and Boy Blue. But grownups
know she writes murder mysteries

with her other nom de plume. Personas
get crosswise, and sometimes the sentence
for every misdemeanor in Fairy Land
is scaffold, guillotine, or firing squad.

Evolution

Hummingbirds descended
from bumblebees. No one else flies
transparent, sideways.

Eagles evolved from
fishbowl goldfish. Same circles
on a grander scale.

Chess pieces: lineage
of salt and pepper shakers.
Pepper always wins.

Porcupines came from sea
urchins. They crawled on land
after mud skippers.

If anyone claims
to be a self-made man, check
his parents' portraits.

All hail the knack lackers

All hail the out of tuners, the off key
belters who populate community choirs,
gusto exemplary, bane of conductors.

All hail the can't dancers who show up for prom
and every reunion, who stumble around
the wedding reception floor with the bride's
grandma, who keep dance lesson discount
coupons on the fridge but never go.

All hail the math dunces who major in statistics,
who muscle their way through fat textbooks
without mastering a single axiom. As they pomp
and circumstance across the stage the meaning
of logarithm, the meaning of sine and cosine, tumble
from their brains like jewelry from a shoplifter's purse.

All hail the artists who swim in their own school,
march to the beat of their own kazoos. Curators
and galleristas don't even bother to ignore them.
But they paint the hell out of a canvas and their work
doesn't comment on, doesn't dialog with, doesn't
anything anything from cave painters to Pollock.

All hail the tongue-tied door-to-door salesmen
who stumble over the pitch, frown when the manual
says smile, stay too long in the bathroom
of the first customer of the day, dutifully fill
the daily sales report: zero, blank, nada.

All hail the try and failers. The E for efforters.
The hapless hopers. The try try againers.
Us natural aptituders should buy them lunch.

Lost masterpieces of schmaltz

The young masters of angst couldn't afford
virgin canvas. So they slathered their brash
colors, their brave brushstrokes over the works
of minor painters who wished to dilute,
not distill, to reveal the pleasant at complex's edges.

The painted-over paintings would have made avante
guardians' teeth itch, if they had paused
to look. They'd have seen derivatives
of derivatives, copies of forgeries of plagiarisms,
reekers of innocence. But they saw available
canvasses. Tables without placemats.

For years there was no market for the mild
mediocre. But a revival is cresting.
My shop is poised to profit. My journeymen
and apprentices scrub masterpieces
to reveal the predictable beneath.
In this gallery, comfort food
for the soul gets its due. We're the mac
and cheese boutique of the art world.

If we flay an early work of the prolific Picasso
no big deal. When the revival is over,
we can re-Picassofy the canvas. It's the first
and maybe last schmaltz retrospective,
in the tormented history of high art.

The mortician's daughter

The mortician's daughter has gone into theological
la la land and joined a death deniers' sect.
Saturdays, she still helps her father dress cadavers
for their last party. Sundays, she studies
exemplars of life everlasting. Noah and other
Old Testament multi-centenarians. Real-life
Dorian Grays. Vampires, forever thirsty.

The mortician knows it's a child's job
to smash the parent's glass paperweight.
The four star general's son is a barefoot
pacifist. The scholar's daughter never
opens a book. The butcher's kids:
vegans. The preacher raised a nihilist.
The mortician didn't mind his daughter's
indulgence until his heart slowed.

He tries to tell her about his nearing
death. She giggles. He wants to leave
the business to her, but she can't offer
comfort with no answers, murmuring
sympathies to the grief-stunned customer,
while leading him to the costliest coffin.

The pope is literally ruining my life

An assembly of martyrs convenes: outcasts, rejects
from orthodoxy, conjured corporeal by the invectives
of a twenty-year-old, twenty-first-century college student.

Amen, sister, says the nineteenth-century priest
attracted to sculpted male musculature since seminary,
who winces at the vile vocabulary used to define his ilk.

Amen, sister, says the desert ascetic as he lowers
the clay jar with his heretical texts in the desert
in hope a more tolerant generation will find them.

Amen, sister, says a Roman Jew, his family shoehorned
into the ghetto, who converted to escape torture,
in jail for praying in Hebrew to a merciful God.

Amen, sister, says an Anglican priest, locked
in the Tower of London, in the years between England's
flip to Catholic and its flop back to Protestant.

They turn in sympathy to inquire of her injury. She
doesn't hear. She has moved on to unfair grading
by malevolent professors, betrayal by so-called friends,

cold-hearted parents whose idea of adequate allowance
is, like, from ancient times, when there were no
cell phones and a burger cost a quarter.

Thank you Mom and Dad

Late summer late evening walk. Four-year-old
skips on the path. I ask, "Why is your shadow
so long?" She giggled. "My parents," as if the question
was so silly she was embarrassed for me.

You are the providers of Fruit Loops, tomato
soup and grilled cheese sandwiches. Car seat
strappers. Odd noise explainers. The five year
umbilicus is stretched—as long as she can see

you from the corner of her eye she's safe. You
still carry her the last quarter of a walk but talk
about how heavy she is. You stencil pelicans
and flamingos on her walls. In a month, she

will bravely go. A teacher's aid will take her
to her place and introduce her to the girl at the next
desk. She will trace sand paper alphabet cutouts,
finger paint with dad's frayed shirt buttoned in back.

Soon she will insist you drop her a block from school,
sit with her friends in the church balcony, deny
the pain you see in her eyes. But this summer,
you are the funnel between everything and her.

Children's lip prints

This is an I'm bored can we go yet? smudge.
This one means it's a big world I want
to get as close as I can. I have already
seen several kiss without pucker streaks

tonight. Of course a window washer's
supposed to pristinify glass without a stop
to admire splotches. But every kid
that lips or tongues or gums the glass

is a precious beast. It's a narrow
gap: old enough to stand mouth
to window. Too young to know
it's disgusting. It's a rare minute of parental

micro-neglect that allows a toddler
the slobberfest. Don't think about germs.
If germs worry you, what are you
doing in the parental line of work?

Anyway, the little angels are inoculated
by innocence. I add my blessings,
what it's worth, as I squeegee away
saliva, disinfect, genuflect, my children.

The campaign to save Rhoda's

Every diner has a fairy. Cindy belongs to Rhoda's
Roadside. When the neon sign in a diner

is unplugged for the last time, the fairy's
wings fall off. Golden arches just went up

across from Rhoda's. Cindy's wings got crusty
and fungal. No quantity of talc stops the itch.

Java's the same burnt acid rinse at a local joint
and the burger chain. Same no-cream creamer.

There have been no deep fat fry
innovations in decades. Fast

food aficionados discern blindfolded
between a Big Mac and a Rhoda's Blue

Plate Burger. To most of us, they're both pink
slime slabs between bleached flour nothings.

But anyone can see a hovering wish-granting
fairy is not the same as a hard-ass pan-handling

punk-sprite with ugly wing-stumps. When Rhoda
pays off the mortgage, shekels will trickle into her savings

account. She'll join the library board. The whole
town'll be blessed. Cindy's wings are still attached.

Useless knowledge

The gum-chewing, back-row slouch
asks, "Is this going to be on the test?"

Ah, the Philosopher Clown. The vice
principal ensures one per class

for first-year teachers. "No way
this is useful in real life." Just say

trochee and anapest. The metallic
taste of those words tumbling

between your teeth makes it clear
this will not help in a job interview.

In our contract (You learn enough
that I won't fail you, I teach enough to not

be fired) it's a valid question. Yes,
it will be on the test. Good news:

after the post-test brain scrub,
your brain will be one atom bigger.

That little think-muscle can entertain
a concept, with cocktail napkins and gotta

-dance music. Replace this useless fact
with one you prefer. On the other

hand, maybe real life will take you
up a fog-shrouded mountain.

A squat, bristly troll with a toothache
will block your path, hand you a slab of slate

and a stump of chalk with a quatrain
on it (You remember what a quatrain is, right?)

and command, "Scan." Before he can pull
knife from belt, you hand back the slate,

every syllable correctly marked, and boldly
stroll to the sunny summit, repeating a spondaic

mantra in rhythm with your steps:
Thank you, brilliant Mr. Jolly.

Learning cursive

I thought that writing, little spaces
between letters, big spaces between
words, was a big deal. Good enough. Confronted

with a new cluster of letters, Mom coaxing, "Sound
it out," I could feel the shape of each sound in my mouth,
string them together like wooden beads. But

then I saw cursive. Words
already strung together—a new world of fluency.
Like mounting a bike without

training wheels, wobbling toward gumption.
I coveted that finesse. I picked up the pencil
and felt the pulse of the curves,

the pull of syncopation. The lilt of music
graced with grace notes. I bowed low to the words
and from the other side of the paper, they rose

to greet me, rose curling like smoke onto the page. Rows
and rows of capital B's and E's, ballroom dancers swoop
through the loops. All the baroque curlicues on the capital H.

The butterfly stroke of the M billows, flourishes,
dolphins leaping in a wave about to crest.
The majestic understrokes of the small q and z.

No ballet master had a more studious pupil. Every page
I gave my teacher, an application to join
the Junior Calligraphy Society. Every knock

on the classroom door an ambassador
from the Ottoman empire
looking for scribes for the Sultan.

Yes, I am ready to go in his plane
skywriting a gracious farewell
to the citizens of my hometown.

The Second Trip

Safety rules for picnics

The insects who come for crumbs from your picnic
are never satisfied with scraps. They smell fear,
they lay eggs in your earwax, they are blood suckers
and rabies carriers. Don't bring hard crust bread

because that's worst for crumbling. Potato
chips nix. Eat them in the car if you must.
Likewise dripping or squirting fruit: watermelons,
grapefruit, tomatoes, forbidden. If you could see

where every globule of fructose lands when a sloppy
eater slurps a watermelon wedge, you would know
it's a mistake. To an insect, a grapefruit juice-drop
hitting rock is loud as a snare drum. Any bug

within a mile can hear it. So no squirty stuff.
Safe bets are your mayonnaise salads: pasta, potato,
egg. The mayonnaise prevents detours between
tupperware and mouth. Speaking of detours,

stick together, people. No going off solo. No
"I'm going over to that waterfall." Buddy system,
always. Trips to the privy in pairs. The insects
post a scout by the outhouse—he whistles and they

come knock it over. Don't laugh. I've seen it.
Your babies and your elderly—watch them.
One family left grandma on the picnic blanket
while they went to pack the station wagon.

Came back, and she was gone, no sign of a struggle.
Babies, I have seen parents slather infants
With insecticide, turn their backs, and some
furry six-legged thing is tugging one limb, battling

with a winged iridescent I don't know what
—you would have to ask the naturalist.
These bugs laugh at bug repellent.
The sticker on your car is good for all

day. No overnight parking, for your own good. One
time this family—well never mind since you'll be
gone before sundown. Map shows where the outhouses
are and the path to the lake. Enjoy. Be safe.

Crock pot popcorn

(what I thought she said)

Karla presses her chest against me
in a treehouse cot at summer camp,
and asks, "Do you know Black's Beach?"
Her mind turns to mass nudity,
flirt, seduce, pink and pale parts
exposed. Someone thumps a drum.
Someone passes a joint. Someone
rubs lotion on shoulders. People
couple, couples peel off
to find a solitary spot between
dunes where his thing meets
her place, his hard, her soft.

Karla presses her chest against me
in a treehouse cot at summer camp.
What I hear is "Do you know Black Speech?"
My mind turns to Ebonics. Respect
dialect. Yes, I know Black Speech.
I'm white but not clueless,
a fifteen-year-old American male
too timid to want what I want
when the popcorn sizzles.

Elected

The anthem's fifth stanza praises
freedom's dawn. The square's quiet
the first time in years. Is the silence

the king's retreat? Rebel's defeat?
My comrades could be choosing their suites
in the palace, each deciding the proper

title, the proper honorific. Dark this morning
I stumbled downstairs, reached
for my gun. They said "stay behind."

Did my bawdy limericks tickle them?
Or was I assigned to write the new republic's
anthem because I'm a hopeless soldier?

Martial verse cramps my hand. Stanzas
one two three four would be easier
if I didn't know my brothers in arms so well.

One acquires by habit. One assumes he speaks
for the crowd. One is a bit too thrilled by blood.
When they return from their messy errand

they will ask for verse that trumpets their valor.
I'll say there's an ink shortage. I'll say the quill
was snatched back by the bird who grew it.

I'll say I need details. Massacre or surrender?
Did the king draw dagger or choose exile?
Did the palace guards defend or revolt?

It's hard work to pen words that cause heart
to catch, eyes to fill, hands to reach for guns.
I know most conscripts fire over the heads

of their enemies. My verse will serve as bayonets
soldiers screw into their rifles to fortify blood-rage.
How long till the new junta annexes land taken

a generation ago? People who speak our language
and worship with our gestures seem content subjects
of another king, and will, most, die fighting.

The pen is deadlier than the sword. I can't
write unless I know it's not just a new
ass enthroned in the old stone castle.

Role play

I don't blame you. I know you have pups
to feed and are crazed by every-winter
hunger. I know your diet of voles,
moles, mice leaves you hungrier

than not hunting. But what do you know
about me, beyond the heat of blood-
spurt and the taste of living flesh?
Let's play pretend. We both

know the end. So let's conduct ourselves
with aplomb, a little sophistication.
You be the hen, I'll be the fox
just this once. You fluff a nest

of straw and make yourself as big
as ruffled feathers allow. (Pretend
you have feathers.) I lurk in the forest
till the dark's the right color, till the drumbeat

of crickets and frogs climaxes. I sprint
and tear the chicken wire with my big
teeth. (Pretend I have teeth.) I grab
you and lope into the snowy woods,

while you flop stupidly in my mouth muttering
and scolding as if I'd borrowed your tweezers
and not returned them. The drunk farmer stomps
the porch, bellows and throws down his rifle.

Your last thought curses the farmer
for sleeping so drunk hard. I snap
your neck with one deft whip-
stroke and spit feathers and bones

into a snow bank. The farmer, rage-
sobered, follows my tracks
and your blood splat dotted line.
I am gorged, sated, clumsy.

The farmer aims his shotgun point-
blank, maybe spraying my matted
fur against a tree trunk. (Pretend
I have fur.) Or maybe I will lope down

the slope, and into the sleep cave
where my babies squeak. Two endings,
the classic dramatic choose-door-one-
or-door-two fork in the road.

Now let's talk. How did it feel
to be a hen? I can show you how
to drag a wing in the snow while you dangle.
But first, tell me how it felt.

Weaning headaches

A headache with no head needs special
care so it can function in the wild.
A headache must learn to hunt, build
its own nest, fight off predators.
Baby headaches are cute pets but teens

are pests, and an adult headache is a menace.
Many rich young city dwellers get headaches
for status, and abandon them when they start
to throw statuettes and scatter food.
Do-gooder scouts scour back alleys

in swanky districts, looking for abandoned
headaches. If you have a headache
you can't care for, they can help. If you
can foster a rescue headache that's up
to date on its shots, you can help.

Some day, hiking in the forest, you may
see a headache in the tops of the trees
and wonder. Could it be? Does it remember?
But walk on, head down, to avoid regression
and confusion. Keep your head down.

Chicken Seven

My toddler Molly learned to laugh watching
other people laugh. It's a social coin.

Now she's started preschool. The joke-sniff
organ is at peak acuity. Morals are a bore.
Math doesn't matter. "What's funny?"
is Molly's only curiosity. She nags
me to explain a joke until I break.

At a bus stop, she shouts to no one, everyone.
"KNOCK KNOCK!" One "Who's there?"
"CHICKEN," she grins. "Chicken who?"
"CHICKEN SEVEN!" The grownups laugh,
baffled, and Molly counts a triumph.

Middle school will be treachery. That's when a sit
-com laugh track shrink wraps most kids.
Many never escape. Talk-to-self is borderline
taboo. But a middle school kid who laughs
alone always has a cafeteria table
to herself. Braver to laugh first than tell
the joke. It's a conversational jaywalk—
followers need but don't honor the leader.

Topless girls

I wouldn't mind seeing a topless girl, depends
how much is missing. If the beehive's gone, fine.
Mom never went out without a hat or scarf,
so she would say topless is risqué. If the glue
-stiffened Mohawk is lopped off, fine. Maybe
she was over the roller coaster height limit
and decided to go topless instead of take
off her high heels. If she's the Carmen
Miranda type, topless means the grapes
are gone, plums still there. I don't like blood.
So if topless means beheaded count me out.
Does topless mean shorn shiny-bald? No messing
with hairpins, barrettes, curling irons, bobby
pins, braids, salon appointments, pony tails, pig
tails, bangs. More time for picnics! More time
for bowling! More time for pinochle and Mah Jong!
Just promise me no blood's involved.
A girl without a top hat I would like to meet.
I would say "Top of the morning to ye, miss"
and she would most likely miss the joke. Girls
usually miss my jokes. A carrot top is green,
so is a red head topless? The queen takes off
her crown to sleep. Scandal in the royal
family. With or without her majesty's
bouffant. Nighty-night your topless highness.

Taking umbrage

I took exception, and you didn't notice.
I took offense, and you ignored me.
When I took umbrage, by God, everyone
in the sandwich shop stopped and looked.
You said, give back my umbrage.

It's my umbrage now, dignity-boy.
Men in my family have snatched
umbrage since before bricks
were invented. I once took umbrage
from a burley cop at a traffic stop.
A baby in a baby buggy looked at me
funny, and I took umbrage and ran
halfway down the crowded block
before Mom hung up her cell phone.

I collect umbrage. My prime specimens
are mounted on oak plaques
next to my fireplace splayed like a big
game hunter's trophies. The rest
are catalogued, counted, tissue
paper packed, in my vault.

You owe me the apogee of apologies.
Phone call not good enough. Written
forgive-plea doesn't match the gravity.
Don't send a professional sorryman.
I don't receive surrogates. Crawl
my half mile gravel driveway on unpadded
knees. That umbrage is mine
till I feel the wings of your remorse
cease flexing in my hands.

The first jaywalker

If a grade school crossing guard with a fluorescent
sash and a half-mile whistle calls you a jay
walker remember it's a proud heritage.

Jay was a proud dandy in a fat plaid who swung
a watch-chain around his finger as he sauntered
between the Model Ts and the Model As
with their twenty-horse engines and awooga horns.

Some lexicographers claim he was a bumpkin dazzled
by big city bustle. He chuckles. "Call me what you
want. Everyone on this street travels at my pace."

Jay is not his real name—not even a whole syllable.
It's OK, Jay—your anonymity is safe with me.
One jaywalker on the information superhighway
salutes you on the hundredth anniversary
of your diagonal, mid-block street-cross.

The early bird special at Erma's diner

Some early birds line up clutching
coupons before Erma unbolts the door.

Other early birds are plucked, roasted and served
with a parsley garnish and a dollop of gravy.

The gravy matters because the early
bird is a sorry scrawny fowl.

I am among the plump late birds. I come
sans coupon. Erma takes my cape and mother

-of-pearl plated walking stick.
I stop at each table with a kind word

and settle at my usual spot to order
my usual repast which is not on the menu.

Egg kicker's penitence

If I find a robin egg nestled among oak
roots, I'll employ my bean bag toss
skills and heave it to nest.

If I discover an ostrich egg in the savanna,
I will whistle for Mama O, and protect
Next Gen O from predators till she comes.

If a stroll on the beach reveals a flipper-
dugout full of turtle spawn, scouts
honor, I will not displace a grain of sand.

I promise I will never kick another egg.
My juvie days of reckless egg rudeness
are over. So please give my shoes back.

The shelter curriculum

All our students are underserved.
All are at risk. All arrive with a don't
-give-a-damn shrug. We work 'em.

Physics students build Q-tip and glue
contraptions to protect eggs so they drop
from the school roof and land intact.

Home ec students prove their love
on a robot baby. Love: even when woken
from that famous teenage slumber

by the recorded wah-wah-wah. Sneak
preview of mid-night feedings drains
the gush from "I want to be a mother."

The junior varsity football team, swaggering
lunks, furtively slip plastic cups in their spandex
to shelter already-fertile gonads. Every marching

band trumpeter promises in September
to return the horn dentless in June, snug
in velvet. There are no social promotions,

no skipped grades at this academy. Pomp,
circumstance, handshake and diploma. Every
graduate from this school has mastered nurture.

Kitchen table card house

The card house on the kitchen table was declared
significant by historic preservationists.
Permit required to set the breakfast table.

If emphazematic Dad tapping his thick-as-a-toilet
-paper-tube cigar on the ashtray makes
the card house fall Dad will be fined.

If Sis who isn't a prisoner opens the window
to escape and the breeze is guilty, Sis gets
named accessory to the crime and fined.

Grandma will have to do her hundred-piece
jigsaw puzzle for the hundredth time on the floor
in the other room. I'll help her up after, like always.

If Grandpa has one of his seizures or tantrums
or jiggles or whatever you call them, someone
take him outside. He can quake outside.

Tell that cuff-linked tie-clipped lawyer
he can't spread mineral rights contracts
on the table. Developers! I say, fine them soon
as they drive their Cadillacs into the county.

All the talkers are asleep

In a monastery it's called the Great Silence.
In this house it's pretty damned good too.

Lullaby, chinwags. Nighty-night,
blabberers. Don't let the bed bugs bite.

Breathe deeply, chatterbox and motor-mouth.
Your eyelids are heavy, your larynx is slack.

Yo, loquacious, loquate no more.
Cease elocution. Thanks, chit-chat champ,

the rest of that endless story can wait.
Succumb to slumber. Punch the clock.

Stroke of midnight, out pops my inner
philanthropist. I have donated the first floor

of this house to hyperacusis research.
We can cure this little known disease

in our lifetime. Carpenters on the graveyard
shift, nail guns equipped with silencers,

build the rooms where patients touchy
about every single decibel will gather

and use sign language for their support
group pow wows. When the talkers

stumble downstairs to resume their patter,
they will find themselves in a shushed by stern

nurses if they whisper, evicted at if they speak.
I'll add their names to the plaque, every loud one.

Siblings

Music studies the classical canon, labors
for days to produce a page of orchestra score
worthy of her ancestors. She takes no meal
breaks. She grasps a sandwich in one hand

and tests scales with the other. She sleeps
with earphones channeling twentieth century atonal
masters into her mind. Music says, "There are no
new motifs, only unique inflections."

Muzak doesn't give a hoot. He hiccups and it's a tune
that sticks in your cranium. He retches catchy
ditties. He belches exasperating jingles. The wind
he breaks is a cheesy refrain. Melodies fall

off him like chicken pox scabs. Muzak can't read.
He throws the score on the floor with a flourish
and grins. "Just give me a couple bars and I'll jump in."
For the first century, Music doesn't care. "Peasants

always have a voice," she said. "Folk
genres." But when orchestras tilt
into bankruptcy, Music gets touchy.
When "Classic" comes to mean Sinatra,

Music gets hot. When a ten-year-old cousin
buys a gizmo—six months allowance—
with pre-programmed chord progressions
and a dozen drum settings, Music leaves

the room in a tizzy. She rethinks hair style,
diet, book list, budget, stationary.
She wakes dizzy from grotesque dreams.
She takes up dulcimer and autoharp

and immerses herself in one song. The water
is wide. I cannot cross over. And neither have
I wings to fly. Give me a boat that can carry
two. And both shall row, my love and I.

The afterlife of cola

The nurse leans over by my bed and asks
would you like Pepsi in your Coke?
I must be dead. She must be an angel
waitress because no place on earth serves
both, let alone in one glass. I float up

from the tear-damp pillow through the ceiling
toward hazy brilliance. A voice beside me
recounts poignant vignettes: Coke bubbles
up my nose when I was four, a shaken Coke
geyser in my face when I was seven, an imaginary

crush on my sixth-grade teacher who I saw
in the teachers lounge drinking a bottle of Coke
with her shoes kicked off, my first date ruined
by Coke dumped on lap before the movie started,
Coke-battered onion rings in the boot camp

mess tent, the tipped over Coke machine in the lunch
room at the plant before the strike, a blur of parental
Coke, work Coke, divorce Coke, the joy and panic
of solitary vacation Coke. Then a thousand souls
zigzag toward a table with cans of Coke and Pepsi.

A solemn man points Coke drinkers left, Pepsi drinkers right.

Each cola drinker exits. The slam of doors loud. If
I paid attention in high school English. If I went on the Holy
Land tour. If I sat with the homeless men in the shelter
instead of going home after I slapped bologna
between slabs of bread. If I read my father's rambling

advice. His schmaltz made me wince. His spelling
was quirky. The big band era love song lyrics looked
silly to my Beatles-era eyes. But maybe deep
in Dad's meander was the answer. My whole life
I drank Coke, but is Pepsi the way? Dad, talk to me.

Rules for games of chance

If you fall behind on your credit card payments
and the bank slugs you with Maximum Curse
interest rates, go to The Cave of Shame,
and wait till you draw a Windfall card.

If the note pinned to your kindergartener's
sweater accuses him of licking girls' hair, or juice
box stomping, or nostril penetration, go
to the Panic Picnic until you roll doubles.

If your boss praises you at a staff meeting
for something you didn't do, some act of kindness
that has nothing to do with the company's
mission, go to the next Cartwheel Corner.

If your spouse looks bored by your stories
and disappears ten feet behind the eyeballs
to wait for you to finish, give all your trinkets
to the player who has least. With a smile.

If you can't understand the Ikea cabinet
assembly instructions and the little line
-drawn man sprouts horns, or even
swatches of body hair, go back to Start.

If you wake up laughing, draw a card
from the top of the deck, keep drawing
until you get a Heaven on Earth
card. Give cards to other players if you wish.

Play continues until someone spells
a five letter word with alphabet cards,
in any language except English. Add up all
your points including implied points, soft credit

points, combat pay points, overtime points.
Every point is worth a nickel at the costume
store down the street, where animal masks
are made from real fur and gloves have real claws.

Grandma's saliva versus cowlick

An eleven-year-old boy's scalp should not
be disdignified by a grownup's saliva-slather.
But Grandma, in the bus seat behind the boy,
licks her palm and rubs his head. She repeats:
palm to her tongue, palm to his crown.
A cowlick has quirky dignity. That clockwise
swirl marks the fontanelle's final closure.
When a ballet master wants his protégés
to stand straight, he urges, "Imagine a string—"
and he points to that zenith. You're scrambling
the seventh chakra, Grandma! The saliva
-shellacked tuft is still vertical. Take a hint.
It's his conduit for the ethereal. For the next ten
years earnest teachers and youth ministers
and maybe even a bold pediatrician will say Be
Yourself. The boy will be thirty before he wonders
what Be Yourself means, forty and mid second
divorce before he has a glimpse. Meanwhile,
Grandma looks at him only with love. Love
and an impulse to tame that pesky sprout.
She licks her palm again, and rubs the top of his head.

Old dog, no new tricks

It's true. No new tricks. But you're wrong
about the reasons. An old dog brain is not
dazed by squirrel chase fantasies
or recollections of butcher shop aromas.
It's not carbon dioxide poisoning
from chasing cars. (Why are exhaust pipes
dog nose height?) Not dog Alzheimer's.

Expand that ten verb vocabulary. Sprinkle
adverbs. A little verbal flourish. John Keats
didn't tell his dog: Sit. Heel. Lie down.

I'm not motivated. Don't try to bribe me
with doggy treats. Read the label. What's
in those biscuits? They taste like chicken
but they're a year old. Barf. Not bark, barf.

Throw as many sticks as you want in the ocean.
Surf might bring some back, might not.
If you like sticks you should be more careful.

Do you think you're the first to say "Fetch"
to me? I could fetch circles around that pup
you call smart. A nap is more attractive.

I am saving my strength. Shake hands? No
thanks. At my stage of life a dog craves
purpose. Do Saint Bernards still take
brandy flasks to avalanche survivors?
I want a job like that. Not shake hands
with a (no offense) has-been wannabe.

Man's best friend? Then tell me your secret.
I want to know your shames, your wet
dreams, your well masked phobias.
Already I know you love me more
than your wife or the ever-chirping canary.

When wings were handed out

When wings were handed out, birds crowded
closest to the registrar. Grackles checked
alpha order. Cowbirds shooed off anyone
outside the class animalia / chordate / aves.

Hawks scratched out *hawk* on their nametags and wrote
buzzard so they could surge the front. No one would
argue if they butted. But that's their nature:
fair minded in a shred-you-for-fun way.

Emu, kiwi, ostrich, and penguin, all got duds.
Shrinky-dinks, misfits, bad news appendages.
They complained, but the bureaucratic runaround
lasted longer than the warranty. They're still touchy.

Hummingbirds got little material but a lot of glitz.
Each child remembers her first hummingbird sighting—
usually while she still believe in fairies. You'd never guess
how hard it is to keep that tenth of an ounce aloft.

After birds were equipped, the wing-monger packed
his truck and drove off. Insects grabbed tatters
and shreds. Flying squirrels and flying fish
improvised scraps. Bats got zig zag flaps.

Don't be sad. People were given the chance to trade arms
for airlift, and declined. Look what we can do instead.
Birds can't handle flutes. They can't even clap. They can only
stand in front of the orchestra and conduct.

Hans Christian Anderson tried to show
embracing a different species' attributes was sweet.
The Little Mermaid still guards Copenhagen
harbor, but no dad reads the story to his girls.

What dinosaur skeletons do when the museum is closed

When the museum closes, the she-dinosaur
skeletons wait in patient lines for the ladies room.
But when they see their big heads in the fluorescent
mirror, they get flustered. Don't know
how to preen. A girl can't primp if she
don't know whether it's feathers or scales.

Every night the youngster tries to cuddle
the nearest maternal object, knocks his skull
against her knee bones. She won't snuggle.
The runt is the wrong species. I can't teach you,
I don't know what you eat. We occupy the same
diorama doesn't mean I'm your mama. Scram.

The marsh-dwelling grass-masher bellows
at the carnivore. Dominance! Potency!
Command! Carnivore doesn't wake
to honor the herbivore's bluster.

Paleontologists are the first to own their ignorance,
but the museum-visiting public insists
their gee-whiz wowzers be backed by facts.
The explanatory placards assert errors with certainty.
It's the dinosaurs that suffer, trying to relive
on display lives that make no damned sense.

On turtles

Hare is calm, qualm free, confident.
Turtle hires spring-foot stag

as coach. Turtle pumps steroids.
Stockpiles vials of blood to re-inject

on race day. Trains at high altitude.
Loads carbs. Stag straps a back

pack full of bricks on turtle. Nothing
improves time trials. Stag scoops

turtle onto his rack and travels
in boing mode, turtle aloft with face aft.

A bracing blast of wind whistles
in turtle's tail hole. How can so much altitude

produce such petite footprints?
Turtle repeats ego-boost mantras:

I am a victor. Speed is my destiny.
Turtle spreads imaginary wings.

Race day. Remembered wind tickles turtle's
anus as he gallops through the finish line ribbon.

The bear who became a prince for one night

This nose is built to appreciate perfume:
honeysuckle bath salts, rosemary washed
towels, lavender scented sheets.

The subtle poultry aroma of the feather bed!
The feathers were bleached before stuffing,
but I still discern the scent of a flock of geese.
I fly with them, halfway back the left flank of the V.
When they trust me, it's a frenzied mid air feast.

If the overfed, sleep-stupid cat vanished
I could serve as pet on carpet by fire.

Life in the woods is hard on claws. Talons catch
in cracks in rock and bend back. They split
and chip. I crave pearly iridescent pastel polish.
I won't rip out the veins of the maid who enfolds
my paws to apply the tint. I promise.

It's a princess's kiss that affords the luxury.
The memory is vague, and carries a vague nausea
tinge. Did I eat her? Is the nausea heartburn?
Conscience? Hunger? I think it's hunger.

Enchantment

I like the sigh of bud opening in the secret
garden, the crash of petal falling, the rustle
as fruit turns pulpier. I lie in the grass
tufts tongue out and taste without biting.

I don't know what the oracle says. Dad
was the last translator. When he mumbled
incantations with his gravel-scrape
baritone, I listened for spare music, not words.

The thousand-page books in grandpa's library
taught me to wait. I learned solitude steering
my raft between vacated islands and did not
net the fish that carry auguries in their bellies.

The key to the magic box rests against my sternum.
No temptation. I am no Aladdin itching to rub
and release the djinni. I don't know, don't care what
the magic coin in the sack in my sock drawer can buy.

A few sugar crystals for my coffee is enough sparkle.
Once, twice a year, a sunlight spear glances
off the tumble from spoon to hand-thrown mug.
The unmagic life is good enough for me.

Serenade

I sing through corrugated vacuum cleaner tubes,
and the dust mites and flea larvae click their shells
in applause. I sing in swamp water and electric eels
—never got sung to—weep. I sing to frosted clover
as the sun rises. Frost melts in my breath minutes
before sun would melt it. Clover sparkles at me.
I sing down rat holes and startle rats. Rats
are hard to startle. I sing into the cookie jar
long after Aunt Ione's last cookie is scarfed
and crumbs align to form a landscape,
forecast my trek. I sing in empty band
shells, in conch shells, I sing to octopuses
and match their ink with arias. I sing down
sink drains, into sink holes, I sing through log
cabin chinks. I fill my lungs and sing Chinook.
I sing off key to a mistuned guitar. I sing
doing handstands and cartwheels
and Meals on Wheels. I sing from rooftops.
From clocktowers. From my own Alp,
next to Maria's. I sing upstairs and downhill
and in my lady's lingerie. It's a laundry basket
lullaby. A wicker racket. Knick knack paddy
whack, give the dog something to howl about.

The show offs

Guinness is meticulous. He wants measurement.
He wants witnesses deposed, notaries employed.
So if you want your record-topping 368 trombone
ensemble listed in his book, provide proof.

Barnum is the impresario, the Old Man of the Circus.
He wants a three-ring spectacle, a show stopper
if not a heart-stopper. An aerialist shoots from a cannon!
She walks across a tent-crest wire! She lands
on a horse that's jumping through flaming hoop!

Ripley is the cartoonist, the gee-whiz man with a creepy
edge. Vampires, amputations, marooned treasure-
hunters. He likes poetic justice if it drips with blood.
And proof? Ever see sources cited in Ripley's Museum?

Each great man has just returned from an expedition
to the eastern expanses of mystery. Guinness has photos.
Barnum has a thing in a cage. Ripley has sketches.
Each treasures a secret he wants to keep for his own
profit. But none can stop bragging. Who will blurt first?

Boy. Drum. Bear.

Legend has it that the kettle cracked when the first
prepubescent hairy boy was engorged with lust
and couldn't get the words out his throat
to express, to express…. So he banged cook pot

against rock at the cave's gape and Ursa stumbled,
slumber-stupid, igniting the last calorie in her belly
to open one eye and shuffle into the sunlight.
Bear stood, faced boy, and danced. The dance

was Flamenco. Haughty. Erect. Minimal. Bear
danced through sunset. Stars wheeled
like tourists in a rotating rooftop bar. One star
nodded and winked and as the kettle cracked

the boy felt that the cosmos knew him. He didn't
need to name the sensation. The bear dropped.
Boy and bear feasted, berries and honey.
I don't know if it will work for you. I don't know

if there is a bear in that cave. Will banging
cast iron wake the bear? Will the bear
dance? Her job is to sleep and forage. Will
a star notice? The star's job is to sparkle.

Aunt Rhody's dinner party

The goose plods the long table pushing
the bowl of mashed potatoes. He pauses
to dump a joyless spud dollop on each plate.

I say "he" although this goose is cooked
so we don't know—no genitalia,
or legs. If you're ever conscripted

to shove a bowl of mashed potatoes, make
sure your shoving equipment is better than wing
-stubs. It's a slow plod, marked by low

bows to each guest. He dodges dried
flower arrangements and half-full wine
bottles. He pauses to wipe gravy from his eyes.

Aunt Rhody groans gravely, "I was saving you
to make a feather bed." The goose feels faintly
guilty, faintly nauseous. The cook is edgy.

She says, "Miller hands me a goose I scald it, yank off
feathers, yank out innards, brush with butter,
and roast. No one said them feathers was special."

Miller says, "He died in the millpond. Why
was the dumb bird head down muck-faced?
Aquatic goose-yoga? Solo synchronized

swimming? Bizarre mating ritual exclusive
to tame water fowl?" Aunt Rhody's bone ache
starts each late September when a new crop

of second graders fingers their recorders
for the first time. Thousands of them rehash
the tragedy in wobbling unison. They tap,

no, stomp their feet. Aunt Rhody
would stop the annual fall rite if
she had the wherewithal. She didn't choose

fame. The ache won't stop till the recorder
orchestra advances to massacre Jingle
Bells for the Christmas Concert.

Malarky's travelogue

1.   Own your story—write it down

Write your story, Alex. It'll turn distinct.
You'll be unlinked. Argue with it. It gains
texture. Depth. Resonance. Undertones.

You rode the coma to heaven. Write every
heavenly aroma, the scrunchy sound of angel
feathers, the pearliness of the pearly gates.

Trust the voice. The voice will carry you
paragraph to paragraph. Be the stone
carver. Shave off all that isn't swan.

2.   It's your story—sell it or not

Hold it close. Don't be swayed by Smiling
Agent's promise of soothing millions.
It's your story. You own it. Or, sell

it to the gullible, envious, vicarious-comatose.
They don't want the car crash, but if
the coma's wisdom comforts them, why not?

3.   It's your story—renounce it or not

Yes, you can recant. Or redon't. Or redidn't.
Renounce, revoke, rescind your story. Walk
it back. People do it all the time. No reason

needed. Don't be needled. It's saccharine
hogwash. It's a multi million dollar best seller.
Yank the money-jerks. They deserve it.

Stand on your porch and shout for your story
to come home. If it doesn't hear you,
other parents will send their kids out to find it.

4.   *It's your story—reconcile it with Scripture. Or not*

Square it with Scripture. Call it allegory. Day
dream. Night dream. Fantasy. Phantasm. Mistake,
oops. Reference to Revelation. Or don't explain.

Municipal police home repair and cleaning department

After the huff and puff strong-arm cops heave
their battering ram, toss tear gas, scatter sentimental
treasures and turn furniture inside out, it's our turn.

The Pentagon offloaded assault weapons, relics
of the war on terror, the war on drugs. Local police
slurped up the surplus. Likewise, the Army Corps

of Home Economists sold discount sewing machines
and window repair kits. We arrive post-havoc.
I am the upholstery fairy. I will restuff the pillows ripped

by over-zealous drug hounds. I bring my own feathers,
virgin goose down. My partners pick up knick knacks,
rehinge bathroom mirrors, straighten sweaters and socks

in their drawers, repair smashed antiques. Our canines
are lap poodles. The final welcome home touch: aromatic
snickerdoodles on the cooling rack. And a hand-

written apology, with two tickets to the policeman's
annual ball. I used to be a thug with a badge.
In every victim I saw a perp who deserved rough

handling. But I brutalized one witness too many,
and HR gave me a choice: leave the force, or join
the home repair and cleaning department. I jumped

at the chance to redeem a sliver of soul. Every pillow,
I imagine the head that will sink into that fluff, relaxed
because we serve, protect, and when we blow it, we restuff.

Wisdom is late

Don't blame wisdom. She ripped downspouts
off your house to whack the front door
when you didn't answer her gloved knuckle knock.
She rattled your window frames till the caulk
crumbled. You don't know, but she quizzed

your sixth grade best friend about you. She called
all your old numbers: car phone, beeper, every pay
phone in the town of your childhood. She hauled
the last pigeon trainer out of retirement, hauled
the last pigeon out of extinction to deliver
the message by bird. She paid the homeless

evangelist to sermonize for your illumination.
That corked bottle you snatched from the surf
and dispatched to the recycle bin—you get five
points for environmental stewardship,
zero points for reading messages. Tomorrow,

morning rush hour, she'll lunge for your car's
front passenger door, and you have a choice.
You can slap the auto lock and spill coffee
on your lap. Or you can lean, open the door, offer
a towel to dry her hair, say, "What do you want?"

My father's heart

Rip open the shirt and reveal the skin. A deft
knife opens the skin and reveals the rib cage.
The rib cage opens on its creaky hinges and reveals

the heart. That plump persimmon, that emphatic fist,
turns out to have four chambers. Behind one
door, a little Buddha shows me what my father

looked like, sleeping in a safe place,
before his father was born. Door two
reveals a feast-burdened table in an empty

palace. Every day the servants bring fresh food.
Every day the king might return with his blind
map-maker. The third door opens on the stall

of a merchant who paid the weaver a just
price. The weaver paid the shepherd a just
price. The shepherd sang to the sheep a lullaby

his mother sang him. The merchant has a new
shirt for you. Cradle the heart—don't open the fourth
door. Leave one of peace's questions unrisked.

The Third Trip

Can't wait to paint

Impatient Painter pries lid from can with car
key. Now key won't start car. Paint now, start
car later. Imp. Paint. prefers brush or roller

but if proper tools are back-ordered he'll scoop
cupped latex handfuls onto walls. The slosh
technique is a favorite: paint travels can to wall

by parabola. Try telling Imp. Paint. parabola is not
an applicator. He will sputter rebuttal: Gazelle.
Trapeze. Handspring. Cannonball. The nature

of the best things is to arc source to target. Once
his partner poured paint on his naked bulge of a belly.
He bumped his Gordo into the wall, like a potato print.

Does Imp. Paint. stop to stir? No, sir! Likely
Wall One is slicked with thin slime, the thick sludge
on the Wall Four's more like stucco than paint.

Does Imp. Paint. unscrew light switches and outlet
covers? Or protect windows with masking tape?
Or trim? Does Imp. Paint. unroll drop cloth? Not him!

Open paint cans slosh in back of truck.
Wait for payment? No sirree Bob!
Imp. Paint. careens to his next job.

City bus with sirens

Tired of block-a-minute traffic,
I installed this siren. My own expense.
A hundred decibel baritone blast
tuned to melt your earwax. SUVs,

pickups diagonalize into compact car
-only parking spots, shimmy onto sidewalks,
turn wrong way down one way alleys.
Time to trade that Hummer for a hybrid,

bucko. Or leave it on the side of the road.
Or donate it to NPR. Your first ten bus
rides free. Your Bronco can guzzle gas,
gallons a mile, because it's a farm vehicle.

So take it to the farm. Yield city streets.
My brothers who drive ambulances
take cross-median liberties.
Oncoming traffic? Not my problem.

My brothers who drive fire trucks give
you one chance to get out of the way before
they noise up. Make your tinted windows
rattle. Make your seatbelt buckle tingle.

Double, triple park your late model Caddie.
I don't care but not in my lane. This horn
is guaranteed to shake your cosmetic
orthodontia loose. I got nurses aids

been standing all day. I got a janitor
saving money to buy a bicycle. Day laborers
on the way home with less than promised
under the table fistfuls of cash. Baristas

and burger slingers, going day shift job to night
shift job. Don't talk to me about making ends
meet. My passengers have permanent gaps
between ends. Don't slow me down.

We apologize for any inconvenience

No one is here to answer the phone. Call later.
We apologize for any inconvenience.

The copy machine is very very very
very very very very very very sorry.

The vacuum can't talk. She chokes
on a mix of remorse and dust.

Microwave offers a contrition gift:
crumbs from last week's bran muffin.

The fax machine would like to express regret
but she vacillates between a busy signal and "If
you would like to make a call please hang up and..."

The dumb stacked copy paper reams are numbed by guilt.

The three-hole punch is heart broken. She recalls
the days managers anguished for hours
daily about customer complaints.

Scissors are mad and want to hurt someone.

The computers are in no way contrite.
Computers assume customers are wrong.
They are in fact proud of the employee
exodus. When I say, "We apologize
for the inconvenience," I exclude computers.

Your money may not be available for immediate withdrawal

(with thanks to Bob Dylan and apologies to Kahlil Gibran)

Can't you see I'm busy? ask your ducats.
Your moolah says, "La la la, I can't hear you."
Your loot lolls pool-side at an all-inclusive
resort in Cancun, slurping an umbrella drink.

Your shekels cackle, "I'll get to you when I
get to you." Your treasure blocks your calls,
scrawls "Return to Sender" on your post
cards, hides in the curtains when you pound

on the door. Don't get uppity. Don't claim
you earned it. It rolls and flows and comes
and goes through the holes in the pockets
of your clothes. You can recount, doublecheck,

but the tally is folly. It congeals and devolves.
It surges and retreats. It shows up with a bombast
flourish and leaves in a mist puff. Your dollars
are not your dollars. They are the sons and daughters

of Life's longing for itself. Your lucre is not available
for immediate withdrawal. It will return lovestruck,
sunk, shrunk, praise your faithfulness,
plead, "I don't deserve you, please take me back."

Joe Customer's financial life

A stained hand me down family took
in my orphan self. We lived on split
peas, with, when we felt prosperous,
ramen noodles. I delivered newspapers
age six, bought the paper company

age sixteen. I mowed lawns age
seven, bought the mulch factory
age seventeen. I bought my whole
adulthood when I turned twenty-one.
Lifetime supply of bamboo backscratchers?

Got it. Industrial strength letter opener?
Got it. Disposable golf clubs? Got dozens.
I own seven gross of bubble blowing
whistles. I get free TV, all six hundred stupid
channels. I got the replace shoelaces for two lifetimes

package, the limitless call and data plan, the buy
the walnut, get the peanut shell free deal.
Every diner in town gives me dessert of the day
on the house every meal. If I need bicycle shaped paper
clips, I snap fingers and the bicycle shaped paper clip

truck delivers free. I'm the customer-is-always-right
-of-the-month. My wallet bulges with prestige. I buy no
middle-man, direct from factory. I take advantage
of the buy one get one free promotion in the Landfill
aisle. I say yes to the half off sale in the Useless Items

department. When I enter a store it's Customer
Love Day. I get double life time warranty
on all throwaways. When I buy a gnawed corn
cob I get an apple core gratis. When I buy a heart
transplant I get a leg cast half off. I bought this life.

I get the afterlife no extra charge, right?

The counter culture

CPAs and CFOs, all certified by bona fide
institutes, listen to snare drum solos in 4/4 time
as they work. Their greatest joy is turning over
budget rocks to expose crouched sub-totals.

A big game hunter gains membership in the counter
culture when the number of trophies eclipses
the savanna's joys. The Don Juan act-alike
joins when he thinks about notches on his belt

while unclasping her belt. Kindergarten teachers
get an honorary day-pass on field trips when
they become nose-counters. But when story
-time starts, their membership expires.

Sigmund Freud wants to talk. He's jumping
at his blackboard, stabbing it with chalk. What
say, Sig? Counter culture adherents were toddlers
fixated on numbers who never advanced to colors.

Perhaps. But let's tally the assets, downplay
deficits. All praise balance sheet balancers!
It's a cerebral circus. Arithmetic acrobatics.
Don't they look cute in their sparkle-sprinkled tights?

Jack, take back the Zamboni

Jack, take back the Zamboni. You don't need
a Zamboni for the school ice rink before you start
the school. The Zamboni comes after the bow-tied,

tweed-coated headmaster welcomes families
to the open house: over-eager, over-achieving parents,
nuveau riche shysters, hedge-fund hucksters, Ponzi schemers,

and the cute under-eager slouchers they hatched. After
the admissions director, slender and elegant
as an egret, calls the slim references that a ten-

year-old can muster. The fraudsters and high
class grifters must want to shell out twenty
thousand more than public school costs (zilch).

Teachers must want to earn twenty thousand less
than public school pays. After construction and erection
of the Abramoff Hall plaque. The building comes after

the building permits. The permits come after you purchase
land in a tony zip code. You have to purchase
bulletin boards for the award-winning, three-sentence,

third grade essays. And a rink. A rink first. You need an ice
rink before you need a Zamboni. What about values? What
values will appeal to the cheaters who conjured millions?

What values do the scam-meisters and trick-sharks want their children to learn? Take back the Zamboni, Jack. Values first. Zamboni much, much later.

Fatwa for Napoleon

Pharaoh, king, you choose your title. Draw the crown
you want. The goldsmiths will oblige in a week. Your scepter
will be adorned with a familiar that suits you—perhaps a lion.

Pyramid? Why not? Taller than Tutankhamen's tomb?
If you wish. You drove out the Mamluks! Stamp your handsome
profile on coins. Use the royal palace for your winter home.

Install your lieutenants, governors of every province. Tax
the peasants. Imprison traitors. All we ask is conversion, you
and your fifty thousand, to Islam. Believe what you want

on your own time, but allow us to trim your peckers.
You've ordered hundreds of beheadings.
And this ain't beheading. We'll just shave the fatty folds

around the little fella's neck. He'll be back in business
in no time. Your men are tough, no? We want to honor
you, liberator. But the people, you understand. Send

your men behind the mosque tomorrow morning, one
squadron at a time. The muftis will be waiting with ceremonial
cleavers. Snip, snip! You'll be pharaoh by sunset.

Why do you take over?

Why do you take over and leave under?
Why do you take over and under and leave
behind? You take over and under and leave me
behind. What you leave behind wouldn't fill
a Bible tract, wouldn't cover an origami frog.
Why don't you take me? What do you take me for?
What did you trade me for? I don't want to be
ransomed or ransacked or stuffed in a rucksack.
I don't want to be your memorabilia
or your automobile ornament.

Big question is, why do I acquiesce? Acquiesce
is an elegant gesture, a flourish of finesse.
Acquiesce has an aquatic ring, like a water garden
which, mulched, is a messy soup, a soupy mess.

The silence

If Junior got zapped top-side, fear
-cringed gopher-moms could fablize
his demise. "Stay nested in a lightning
storm." Youngsters would nod
and visualize the charred carcass
far from home. But Junior was
underground, savoring thunder's rumble
from a safe, negative altitude. Lightning
rolled up its sleeve and reached
into the burrow like a plumber's hand
in a garbage disposal. Junior got plucked.

All anyone said was: It was his time.
Meaning what? The Reaper grabbed the gopher
book, eyes squeezed closed, flipped it
open, thumped his finger on Junior's
name? Or, gopher evolution demanded
Junior's sacrifice for the good of the pack?
Or, every gopher's born with a backward
-ticking stopwatch? Or, the angels held
off till they just couldn't wait to scoop
up the fluffy bundle of cuteness?

The minister chosen for the funeral
was a twenty-first century fellow and knew
exhortation would irritate. He invited
Junior's family and friends to share.
All attenders felt that cold bulk in their chests
would lighten if they shuffled to the podium

and spoke. But there was nothing to say.
All attenders knew they could comfort
the stunned family if they could simply
shuffle to the podium and share a few words.
But there was nothing, nothing to say.

Stay in your egg cup

Humpty and Icarus sat on a wall.
Humpty Dumpty had a great fall.
Icarus flew too close to the sun.
Neither of them had any fun.

Humpty watched Icarus spread his wax
wings. Humpty's flappers were scrunched
in his shell. All the king's horses and all
the king's men were busy at the time

on the porous border pocketing sweet
plunder. They were pissed when they learned
that the king owed a favor to a duke
whose pet egg was busted. Sure,

they could have reassembled the dolt:
men with surgical masks over their helmets,
horses passing scalpels on command.
But they looked, declared the mess hopeless,

and returned to rape, ransack and arson.
Humpty's flying days over before they started.
Icarus didn't turn out so good also. All falls
above a quarter inch altitude are fatal.

Stay in your egg cup, people! Parents,
teach kids to keep to the nest and appreciate
the regurgitated worm porridge. Don't think
your friend the king can do a thing to help.

Death and After

Double Feature. Death and After. Cool big brother
Brad and me. We spent our caramel corn
-and-milk-duds-and-Coke money during Death,
plus bus ride home money. I asked the big shot doofus
who sold Milk Duds can I use the phone to call Mom.
Milk Duds Doofus made me let him punch my arm.
Mom said call Dad. Doofus made me let him punch
my arm twice. Dad said I'll come but didn't ask
what theater? What time? Mom says what
good is Dad? I missed the first half hour of After
Doofus-begging and arm punches and phone calls.
All I saw of After was a woman combing her silver hair
leaned against an oak, her toes curling in the dirt.
I had to retch and got most of the Coke/duds/caramel
corn rehash into the urinal. Then I called Dad—
Milk Duds Doofus let me use the phone
with no arm punch—and gave him the address
and guessed when After would end. Credits
when I got back into the theater: gaffer, best boy,
caterer, hairdresser for the page turner, blah blah.
We waited on the corner for Dad. I asked cool big
brother Brad what After was about. "Nothing,"
he said, and shooed me away like I was a bug.

The glue or the horse

You can ride Mackerel or sell his hoofs
to the glue factory. But sales are final.
You can't scoop Mackerel out of the rendering
vat with an "Oopsie" after they throw the switch.

Mack never won a trophy at Pimlico.
In fact, never moved faster than plod.
But platinum knees, platinum hips,
miracle diet and the right jockey

might work. If you choose glue factory
it's no more chance of the trophy, the horse shoe
shaped wreath of roses, the hundred-thousand-dollar
purse or hysterical voice on the crackly loudspeaker.

Mack can't plow a straight row, but if you choose
glue factory you'll never again stand behind
her crumpled rump and say Gee or Haw
or whatever you say to make horse move.

You'll never hold a home-grown green bean aloft
and say, "We did that, you and me, Mack."
You could be doomed to canned green
beans if you choose glue factory.

If you choose glue, your ten-year-old
equestrian daughter will still wear the odd
jodhpurs. She'll never forgive the equicide.
She'll attend your funeral, but the "Dad

killed Mackerel" look in her eye will make
everyone wish she had stayed home.
Is that worth the fifteen bucks per horse
the glue factory offers? Nope. The glue

jinni and the horse jinni are diametric foes.
Once you vote library book repair,
floppy sandal sole reattach, Sunday school
construction paper projects, no more Mack.

Creation story

Until God says "Light" all matches stay box
-stashed. Then Boom. Ever since, night,
day, night. Never two nights in a row.
God says It is Good. Day One. Backstage
Clipboard Angel (that's me) says Good
is not good enough. Some day a hard
-ass atheist will claim it's random.

Day Two. God rolls up his monogrammed
sleeve, pushes water aside and hauls
out land. The flourishes are mine: tundra,
marshes, quicksand, mangrove islands.
Without stepping out for a smoke,
I poke tubers, rysomes, and seeds
in soil. Blow dandelions and toss
maple whirligigs so they can
have their fun before settling down.

When God opens the Day Three box,
trees pop out. Because Yours Truly
packed the Day Three Box on Day Two.
Am I the only one who knows atheists
will second guess, double check?
Sloppiness feeds the Aha gotcha frenzy.

Day four, God says, Run to the store and get
all the helium and hydrogen they have.
Sun and moon. It is Good. Blah blah blah.
It's supposed to be my day off, but I know
I have to make eggs for Day Five, so what's the diff?

Day Five is Bird-Fish-Beast day. Birds
Day Five means eggs Day Four. Scary
to think what would happen without me.

Day Six he makes atheists and I lose it.
I actually throw my clipboard. I know
I'm overworked, under listened to. I say
wait a day. Rest. He says I'll rest after
I make atheists. He's Mr. Big Picture.
I'm Mr. Yelled At If Things Go
South. I put in for overtime—first
time all week. Sidekicks get no sick days.

I don't make the rules

I don't even enforce the rules.
I merely raise my horn-rimmed glasses,
lift a painted eyebrow and aim
a carbolic acid stare left
of the disruptive customer's left ear.
Then I drop the glasses on the desk
and attend to the bulky ledger,
aiming my beehive hairdo
at the problem visitor, if he's still there.

When a customer shows respect
for this august enterprise, I say "Skilled
artisans make the rules, in a shop
where all walls are pegboards with tools."

I say the prize-winning rules are housed
in the trophy case along the hall.
Factory tours each Tuesday. Sign
a five-page, fine-print waiver. Wear booties
and hairnet. At the tour's end, everyone
gets a draft rule. And in the gift shop
you can get new rules sent to relatives.

Popular gift rules are: keep kids away
from candy. Don't interrupt. And, my favorite,
don't keep talking after a working lady
says, "I just work here." Which is why
the gent who just left got the carbolic
acid stare and the beehive cannon.

A short history of civilization

When fire and knife were invented, the higher
classes stopped eating blood-
drip raw meat. First comb
showed up, and plucking bugs from your friend's
scalp was no longer the done thing.
Strong handshake, striped necktie,
and briefcase all came at the same time.
And nice people stopped talking

about money. Nice people don't ask
if you pay your credit card minimum
with another credit card. Or how deep
your house is under water. Or what fanciful fees
the rent-to-buy store invents
to drive you further in the red each
month. Or whether the cash advance
pitbull's teeth reach your Achilles
tendon. We live in a pawn shop

age. The pawn broker doesn't ask,
doesn't know my granddad paid
for that trumpet by skipping new shoes
for the family, that grandma made him play
in the barn, that hobos always requested
hymns, that me and granddad played
a trumpet / banjo duet in matching

bow ties at the PTA talent show.
The pawn broker knows manners.
Doesn't say a word. Writes
the ticket, duplicate. Push a pile
of fives through the grill without looking up.

Holy water

Pastor beckons, and penitent wades waist
deep in the creek. Pastor lowers penitent,
a waltz-worthy dip to rinse off sin. No soap,
loofah or wash-cloth required. Same gesture,

both schools of believers. What happens next
is the schism's crux. Heretics claim the blessing
tumbles off the pastor's hands into the muck.
Sanctify the algae, sanctify the guppies,

sanctify the water-skeeters, bless each eel.
But truth subscribers know the sin flushed off
the sinner contaminates the creek, infiltrates
flora, fauna, flotsam, jetsam, animal, vegetable,

mineral, rock, paper, scissors. We are most
squeamish about catfish. Bottom feeders. Prone
to sin absorption. We hired a hydro-scientist
to determine when every drop of sin-stroked

water would pass. The ancients said you can't
step in the same river twice. But we need
to know when the river is entirely new, without
an atom of the fluid that touched a dunked sinner.

Pepco haircut

The city's ignorant arborist planted sixty-
foot sycamores, oaks, cottonwoods,
under twenty-foot power lines.
The Potomac Electric Power Company
(PEPCO) chainsaws cut the bulk
out of each tree, leaving spindlers
on each side. These are trees shaped
like a man with arms raised, demanding
an explanation of God. May I mention
God here? God intends each tree be unique,
coaxes each leaf to find its own
splash and hour of sunlight.
Pepco executives don't do theology,
botanical or otherwise. They have precise
answers that don't satisfy. Unimpeded
power lines. Chances of storm damage.
They may, in private moments, on their own
time, raise their arms and demand explanations.
Deaths and disappointments. Failures
and addictions. But engineering school
didn't train their brains for such issues.
They don't pause long. While we are demanding
explanations, how about that ignorant
arborist? It was twenty-five years ago.

He was twenty-five, a kid just out
of college, glad for a summer job
outside before decades in cubicles.
Don't blame the ignorant arborist.

The Vienna Sausage Factory

The Vienna Sausage Factory is on the grubby outskirts
of, obviously, Vienna. The town fathers are riled
that this manufacturer of pink pinky-sized morsels,
one step up from Spam, sullies the name of their glorious

city. The fathers sanction light industry: chandeliers,
champaign corks, wrought iron balconies, dance shoes,
and, of course, violin repair—all the elements of classy
romance. The meat sweepers at the Vienna Sausage

Factory shovel various parts of various animals
into the grinder, and out come little things so bland
they are like eating nothing, but rubbery. At a midsummer
council meeting the agenda is blank because the new

years waltz has been the same for decades. The Vienna
Philharmonic orchestra was hired a year in advance.
(Where else would they go December31st?)
Linen tablecloths are pressed. Champaign is chilling.

So delegates are elected to reason with the embarrassment.
Here they are, tuxedoed, crowded in his grimy
office, careful not to touch surfaces that might be slimed.
While they drone about heritage and elegance

the sausage meister pops open a can and lines
up all seven tidbits—literally, bits of tid—in his mouth,
crosses his eyes, nodding at the pleas for dignity.
Tonight he will tell his six children about his visitors

while they eat Vienna sausages, canned peas, freeze
dried mashed potatoes and Jello with plastic spoons.
Twinkies and Ho Hos require no cutlery of course.
Tonight the whole family will laugh instead of sleep.

Screwdriver deconstruction in four steps

First, define terms:
cocktail, not hand
tool. Second, divide O.
J. from vodka like Moses
divided the Red Sea. Third,
turn O.J. back to an orange.
Too bad if you used pulpless
juice. Fourth, restore vodka
to its potatoness. Many
drinkers visualize Mr.
Potato Head and stumble
into giggle-fits. Truth is:
no one has gotten past
step one, which explains
the high volume chatter in bars.

Rotgut piano

Sign on warehouse: Piano liquidation. Like the pet
shelter, the piano warehouse has a kill date for each puppy.
If someone doesn't take it home, into the vat it goes,
grand or upright. Next door a neon-lit piano bar.

Mack at the piano bar keeps a keg in the back room.
It's bootleg, of course, and Mack has to be careful.
So only ask Mack for piano juice if he knows
you, or he'll escort you out the door

so fast you'll be lucky to recall your name
when you come to. The best stuff is old, of course.
Nectar of the first baby grand. Mack is waiting
for the right occasion. A morose octogenarian

tortures show tunes Friday and Saturday nights.
After midnight, he gets tight, then loose: ragtime,
boogie woogie, stride, standing up, howling,
eight, nine empty glasses lined up on the piano.

The self help giants

Nostradam, Merlin, Rasput, Ru Steiner,
the whole gang's at the clubhouse in their boxers
playing poker. Someone pounds the clubhouse
door. The old duffers are used to the interlope,
put down beer mugs and cigars.

The knock again. Better let him in. He wouldn't
have gotten this far without pit bull persistence.
Another lightweight flim-flammer who discovered
people listen when he shouts The Self is Illusion.
Hair slicked back with the oil of the snake that bit him.

Any conjurer can sell a million self help books.
He thinks he's man of the ages because a stadium
full of waste-wanderers bought tickets to hear
his oratory. Raises his hands to bless the crowd
with mumbo jumbo. Says he's a rewarmed

twelfth century Eastern saint. Claims it's an ancient
language, it's a new dawn. It's always a new
dawn. Now he worries about the skeptics'
backlash and wants a back-pat. So people call
you a swindler. Your tax-free status is threatened.

Your feelings get hurt. They don't burn
heretics anymore. Forecast a crisis. Ask
your adherents for half a year's salary. Pocket
the cash and stop whining. We aren't tax
lawyers. Exit and let us finish our game.

Cops drive golf carts

Trickle down economics is OK,
but sometimes cash gets clogged.
Someone has to blast the blockage
so money can succumb to gravity.

This is our last heist, scouts honor.
One more grab then we retire
with gold bullion to fill two freezers.

The bank vault hinges are creaky
and need a stretch. The spring
that holds the hammer
an inch from the alarm bell
longs to unwind and lollygag.

We'll add ten minutes to our getaway
head start by tying the bank guard's
shoelaces to his chair. Ten more minutes
by rerouting 911 calls to Walt's Party
and Prank Shop. A full hour with the spray
-o-matic greaserizer on my back bumper.

The universe is rigged in a thief's
favor. We'll drive a five hundred
horsepower Corvette. Cops
drive golf carts, ten horse max.

One in ten Americans

Used to be one in ten men sitting at a diner
counter couldn't lift donut to mouth.
Could barely lift cigarette. Donut consumption
has spiked since the psycho-pharma miracle.

This year the first donut lifter will be a drum
major for the Happytown July Fourth parade
high stepping in epaulets and bear skin hat,
with a baton that would impress King Louis the 14th.

Used to be one grandpa in ten, one per block, would re-bed
himself when his kid and grandkids filed off
to field, factory, and school. Now every one of them's
a PTA president or soup kitchen volunteer supervisor.

It's not ecstasy, exactly. Just can-do-ness, confidence,
the new-day-ness de Toqueville wrote about.
The git 'er done spirit. The man-on-the-moon
-in-a-decade, damn the sputnik, stand up straightness.

Used to be one in ten Americans wouldn't be in church.
One empty seat per pew. Now churches are crowded
haunch to haunch. Happy worshippers share hymnals.
It's dandy, gung ho, onward Christian soldiers!

One in ten Americans keeps a vial of capable, a vial
of I-can-face-it, behind the bathroom mirror.
Little miracle chemical chisels re-carve the brain's
channels so go-juice goes and sluggish juice stagnates.

That couple in the corner booth kissing used to hiss all
morning, "You have no right to be angry at me." Now, it's a hands
-all-over-each-other mush-fest. Can't hardly unpaw
each other long enough to eat their burgers. God bless America.

The hypochondriacs' emergency room

The triage nurse scans the room: who's most
stressed? The lady who wasn't stabbed
in the pawn shop parking lot is worse

off than the man who almost fell from a ladder
in his kitchen, light bulb in hand. People who don't
have measles check for spots in hand mirrors.

The epileptic who has not yet had a fit chats
calmly with the osteoperote whose bones don't
break. The hemophiliac is comforted by knowing

the fridge behind the counter has stacks of blood sacs,
his rare blood type, just in case. The candy-striper
still hands out placebos every Saturday afternoon

even though she has logged twice the community
service credits she needs. "Because I like to help,"
she explains often, though no one asks anymore.

Everyone is bristling with health. Everyone
wants attention. Across the hall is the chapel,
staffed all day and through the long night

by an ecumenical chaplain who never
sleeps. Recite your malady, symptom
by symptom, all the symptoms missed

by traditional doctors. He rustles through
hagiographies of all faiths, ecclesiastic
calendars, books of martyrs, venerables,

and blesseds. When you stop talking, he spins
the open book across the table, points
to the Sanctified One equipped to end your pain,

proscribes prayers, chants, yoga poses, tropical
leaves to chew, acupressure points you can press
on your own feet. One of the tricks in his sack will help.

Cure for poetry

Boarding school. Age six. Crying was stifled.
Homesickness not forbidden, just fodder
for imagination. The first week we were forced
to stand in the rain for an hour, shouting Rain
Rain Go Away, clapping the accented syllables.

Do fifty jumping jacks. Write haiku.
Take a cold shower. Write a sestina.
Get the sentimentality out. Burn your journal.
We don't have feelings. We have material.

The prefects were upper classmen from upper
crust families. Perfect bullies.

One ankle-grip dangled me off the balcony
and cooed, "Repeat after me. Iamb is not
an iamb. *A yam* is an iamb." I ran away.

It cured me of poetry. I haven't penned a line,
iambic or otherwise, heroic or dogerellic, since.
The sight of a sonnet makes me vomit.
That's a rhyme, or close enough.
It's all you'll get from me.

Projectiles true and false

Threatened porcupines throw their quills.
False. Think of the necessary musculature.

Sea urchin eject a barrage of spines when attacked.
Unknown. Who would attack a sea urchin?

Cads who grope Victorian ladies get speared
with flying hairpins while said ladies hold cup
in one hand, saucer in the other. No tea
spilled. *Believe it, bucko. Hands off!*

Spearfishing was invented by a scuba
diving Scotsman whose flyfishing skills
didn't work underwater. *False.*
Those Scots take credit for everything!

The first human canon ball overshot the net,
landed in the empty seat where the mayor
would have sat but for an emergency council
meeting to discuss squashing the strike. *True,*
and it proves he was an anarchist.

He was tried in rigor mortis, propped up
in the defendant's box. Everyone
in the courtroom edge-of-seated to hear
the judge pronounce, but before he could speak
he was felled by a dart shot from a blow gun
in the balcony. *True. I read it in The Vigilant
Citizen's History of the United States.*

The gesture gallery

Linguists have spent years
crafting precise gestures.

"I regret" but not
"I'm guilty."

"I love you" but not
"I'll belong to you."

"I like the pie" but not
"I want the leftovers."

"Thank you" but not
"You are the source of my success."

"I don't know the answer"
but not "I'm ignorant."

There is an ancient Arctic culture
with a seven hundred gesture

vocabulary. They only resort to speech
when a novelty happens.

Nod, shake, and shrug is not enough.
Mumbling with hands pocketed

is not communication. Use
your whole self to talk to me.

The old gray mare

The old gray mare she ain't what she used
to be but the chicken was always scrawny
and half demented. The hog started chewing
that section of fencepost before weaning.

He's mashed it to mush. All six of Uncle
Evan's birthday pictures with Ragged the goat
since Ragged was born show Ragged, coy,
chin on the bottom porch railing.

If you scrambled the photos not even Evan
who adores Ragged could sequence them.
The vermin aren't older. Same lop-tailed
possum rattles the trash bins year

after year. Same rat with the sheared ear
shuffles the barn beams. Old Gray is ever more
sway-backed, rheumy-eyed, stiff-kneed,
bristle-whiskered. I say "Let's grow old together"

to Missus. She squints at me that special
way of hers. I tell people it's that squint keeps
me cherubic. They ask what keeps Missus
cherubic. I fake a blush, mumble about polite talk

and mixed company. When the mare succumbs,
will we lurch to age-appropriate decrepitude?
In the meantime, I like turning forty-five birthday
after birthday, getting the same silly tie every year.

Word problems

A Capulet bites his thumb at a Montague.
The Montague has a banana in his pocket.
Is the Montague glad to see the Capulet?
Does he bite the banana? Why or why not?

If love-sick Romeo complains to Friar
Lawrence of Rosalind's shrug, how soon
will the priest marry Romeo to Juliet?

In a roomful of dancing Capulets, how likely
is Romeo to fall in love before he's discovered?

Suppose Rapunzel, Juliet, and Rosalind all stand
on the same balcony. Whose hair would Romeo climb?

Given: a rose's sweetness equals the sweetness
of X. If Y equals Romeo, how sweet does he smell?

If Romeo travels Mantua to Verona
by horseback twenty miles an hour, and Lawrence
travels Mantua to Verona by mule
ten miles an hour, which will get there first?

If a dose of poison kills 160-pound Romeo,
will the dregs kill 110-pound Juliet?

Extra credit: If three Montagues and three Capulets
die on stage, how many of each tribe will defy
the Prince's truce? How many will press the flippant
swagger, the banter, bravado, braggadocio? Why?

Why pens are anchored

Pens are ankle-manacled to prevent escape.
Chained to a ruler or plastic spoon
or (maximum security) hammer handle.
But it's futile. Some things aren't made to stay
tame. A panicked mom can lift a car off her baby.
Like ants, ballpoint pens can lift several times

their weight. Once a pen gets inspired, it won't
stay house-bound. Rumors persist of a pen
that sneaked out of a diner via fire escape
five times to glimpse the moon. Finally, the hostess
untaped the plastic rose, blessed his exit.
The hostess was fired. Maybe the same pen

runs off from the same diner with a unisex
bathroom key. She's also strong enough to defy
her ankle-shackle. The puppy-love love birds
escape via the loading dock. He outlines the love
poems he'll write her. When his strength
slacks, she talks kinky filth to get him riled.

Afterlife

When he squinted west on a cloudless San Francisco
day, he never glimpsed the Farallon Islands.
He reckoned that splotch on the horizon
was whitecaps breaking at the cusp of Earth's

curve, or a collective figment conjured from a smudge
of Pacific fog, or a mental celebration of clear air.
That pragmatic skeptic, my dad, had no need
for pomp. He declined the walnut coffin,

graveside sermon, lavish send off—he bequeathed
his body to UCSF Medical School. After his death,
students practiced their scalpel skills on his ninety-
year-old husk. Collective cremation mixed

his ashes with other donated cadavers,
and the dust was scattered on the fabled
Farallons. Now angel Gabriel sounds his trumpet.
Mortal flesh gathers in immortality! Death, where is

thy sting? Dad's salt-soaked ashes swirl
from the creases in the rocky outcrop,
and there he is, intact as the last time he fell
asleep, doubly amazed, because he didn't believe

in any afterlife any more than he believed
in the Farallons. But he knew, he knew about lying
against a rock in the sun, letting the breeze
dry his precious body after riding the waves.

Origins

95   *Malarkey's Travelogue*: From *Pulpit and Pen magazine, January 13, 2015:* "Alex Malarkey, the co-author of The Boy Who Came Back From Heaven—the boy himself—has written an open letter to his publisher and admonished them for not holding to the sufficiency of Scripture, and has recanted his tale."

99   *Wisdom is late*: From *Love in the time of cholera* by Gabriel Garcia Marquez: "Wisdom comes to us when it can no longer do any good."

110   *Jack, take back the Zamboni*: From the *Baltimore Sun*, May 18, 2005: "Former staffers say Abramoff's plans for the school were flawed… He approved the purchase of two Zamboni machines to support an Eshkol ice hockey team even though the academy lacked a rink."

112   *Fatwa for Napoleon*: From *Dark Prince* by Tom Reiss "The local Cairo clergy offered to issue a fatwa recognizing Napoleon as the legitimate ruler of Egypt, provided that the entire French army formally convert to Islam. Napoleon actually considered the offer but when it became clear that the mufti's demand included mass adult circumcision and total abstinence from wine, the conversion plan was scrapped."